A Walk with God for Graduates

A Walk with God
for Graduates

Tim Gossett

DIMENSIONS
FOR LIVING
NASHVILLE

A WALK WITH GOD FOR GRADUATES

Copyright © 2006 by Dimensions for Living

All rights reserved.

This book is printed on recycled, acid-free, elemental-chlorine–free paper.

Library of Congress Control Number: 2005933732

ISBN 0-687-33296-6

06 07 08 09 10 11 12 13 14 15 — 10 9 8 7 6 5 4 3 2 1

MANUFACTURED IN THE UNITED STATES OF AMERICA

Write Your Novel

The integrity of the upright guides them, / but the crookedness of the treacherous destroys them. (**Proverbs 11:3**)

There's an Arabic proverb that says, "Every day of your life is a page of your history." What do you want the novel of your life to be like? Now that you have graduated (and here I'll add my hearty "Congratulations!"), consider making a list of the top values that you want to guide the rest of your life. For example, you might list *honesty, wisdom, faith, integrity,* or *compassion for others*. When the tough decisions of life come your way, you'll have a guideline for making the best choices you can—and you'll help ensure that you will like the way your novel turns out.

A recent high-school graduate told me what she most feared about her future in college: "I'm afraid I'll make the wrong choices." You will likely experience this fear at some point, too. *Am I choosing the right major? Should I continue to date my boyfriend/girlfriend? How do I avoid getting too caught up in the party scene? What part should the church play in my life now?* Questions like these are tough—and I guarantee that you will take some wrong turns on the journey ahead. But having a "road map" now will make it more likely that you will like where you end up! And no matter what, God will never abandon you on your journey.

Dear Lord, may others see in my life story the One who has guided my life. Amen.

Faith Clichés

The mouths of the righteous utter wisdom, / and their tongues speak justice. (Psalm 37:30)

You've scaled the mountain and reached the pinnacle! You've overcome all the obstacles! You're the best and brightest! You've achieved your dream! You are probably sick of graduation clichés by now. In greeting cards, graduation speeches, and receptions, you've probably heard enough well-meaning-but-pretty-standard wishes. Clichés are a dime a dozen, and we overuse them because when it comes to language, we're often as lazy as a cat in the sunshine. These phrases may hold some truth, but there is little life in them.

Similarly, some people have a faith built on clichés. "God helps those who help themselves." "It was God's will." "There, but for the grace of God, go I." "God didn't move—you did." "Praise the Lord!

There are three big problems with faith clichés. They can be unbiblical and simply false. They frequently don't mean anything to individuals who didn't grow up in a family of faith. And they do little to take us into the depth and mystery and wonder that is God.

Just as writing a good essay without resorting to clichés is hard, building a faith without them takes work. But having a rich language of faith means you've really thought about your relationship with God.

God who hears us in any language, may my words about you be clear, honest, wise, and real. Amen.

Make a New Resolution

Of Issachar, those who had understanding of the times, to know what Israel ought to do, two hundred chiefs, and all their kindred under their command. (1 Chronicles 12:32)

Those who make New Year's resolutions know that it's much easier to make one than to keep one. People who do best at keeping resolutions have a friend who keeps them accountable to their promise.

Friend, here is my constant resolution—and I'm inviting you to join me. Say it with me: "I resolve to be more like the tribe of Issachar." And all the people said, "Huh?"

Issachar, one of Israel's twelve tribes, was full of hardworking farmers. They loved their land and wouldn't even leave it to go to war (see Genesis 49:14-15; Deuteronomy 33:18). Tradition says that the tribes of Zebulun and Issachar made an agreement. Zebulun would take Issachar's harvest to market so Issachar could spend more time in scholarship and scripture study. In a time of deep need, the gift Issachar gave to King David was this: they were the people who "had understanding of the times, to know what Israel ought to do."

You live in difficult, challenging, even chaotic times. The world needs your thoughtful, hopeful vision and energy and insight.

Please, dedicate yourself to the Issachar Resolution. It's among the greatest gifts a faithful Christian can offer the world today.

God, fill me with the desire to know the times, the wisdom to know what to do about them, and the strength to do it. Amen.

Practice Makes Perfect

Put these things into practice, devote yourself to them, so that all may see your progress. (1 Timothy 4:15)

If you have ever tried to master a foreign language, a musical instrument, or a sport, you know well the importance of practice. The Christian life likewise requires practice. Scattered throughout this book are seven spiritual practices that are especially appropriate for graduates.

Spiritual practices aren't about proficiency, though. Rather, they are tools we can use to grow deeper in our relationship with God. As we do them, we find we become formed and transformed, gradually becoming more like Christ.

When you find a Spiritual Practice in this book, devote yourself to it. Regularly—daily, even—find ways to integrate these spiritual practices into your daily routine. There are many spiritual practices, not just those described here, so later you can research and learn others. If you are ready to begin a new chapter in your faith, turn the page and begin today!

Today, God, I offer myself to you. Amen.

Spiritual Practice: Breath Prayer

In Hebrew, the word for "breath," "wind," and "spirit" are all the same. God breathed life/spirit into Adam, for example. Thus, breathing is a way of connecting your spirit with God's spirit. Breath prayers are simple, one-sentence phrases that can be repeated over and over at any time—because, after all, you breathe all day long, roughly 23,040 times a day! All you do to pray one is to say it to yourself slowly as you inhale and exhale. Repeat this prayer as many times as you desire, but say it at least several times.

The traditional breath prayer is "Lord Jesus Christ, Son of God, have mercy on me, a sinner." Most of the short prayers in this book will work as breath prayers, too. But you can also create your own prayers. Here's one simple way.

Step one, choose a favorite name for God: *Creator, Great Spirit, Compassionate One,* or *Lord,* for example.

Step two, tell God what you need, in a short phrase. For example: *Grant me peace; guide me; help me do your will.*

Step three (optional), add another short phrase (as in the previous step), or offer something back to God. For example: *Love through me; Walk through me.* Breath prayers are perfect before tests, interviews, difficult conversations, and other stressful times. The more you pray them, the more they can enrich your life and your connection with God!

Lord, live in me, and love through me.

God's Top Three, Part 1

What does the LORD require of you / but to do justice, and to love kindness, / and to walk humbly with your God? (Micah 6:8)

Have you ever wished you could get a "Top Ten List" of instructions from God? This little list from the prophet Micah is just that, but he quit after three. We'll look at each of these, one day at a time.

Do justice. The sad reality in our world is that millions of people experience hunger, poverty, war, genocide, and other inhumanities daily. Behind all of these is a lack of *justice*—a situation in which the will of God is experienced, a way of life in which the needs of people are of major importance. You have an opportunity to live justly—and to seek justice—every day: Buy products that aren't made in sweatshops. Vote for politicians who strive for peace. Work for companies that don't exploit people. Write politicians to express your desires. Get to know people who experience injustice. Treat all people—even the gas-station cash register attendant—as if they are children of God.

Doing justice isn't always easy. In fact, it's often pretty darn hard. But when we don't live justly, we cause more pain in the world. The world has plenty of that already. Come on—make a real difference. After all, it's on God's Top Three list!

Compassionate God, be my guide through the injustices in life. May I bring hope, not pain, to your world. Amen.

God's Top Three, Part 2

What does the LORD require of you / but to do justice, and to love kindness, / and to walk humbly with your God? (Micah 6:8)

You know how there are certain words you use with your friends that would be a little difficult to translate for your average adult? The Hebrew word translated as "kindness" in the verse above is like that. (The word is *chesed,* and it's pronounced with one of those throat-clearing sounds in the first syllable.) It's a word that combines the concepts of loyalty, faithfulness, and love. Whereas justice relates to your relationship with those who are poor and oppressed in the world, *chesed* is the key element in your relationships with those you know and with God. Because God loves us with steadfast love, we are to show that sort of lovingkindness to others.

Now, it's your turn to translate that little bit of Hebrew in your own life. What does that look like in your relationships with your family? with your friends from school? with God? Would your life be a good entry under *chesed* in a visual dictionary?

Kindly remind me, God, not to be just "kind of" loving. Amen.

God's Top Three, Part 3

What does the LORD require of you / but to do justice, and to love kindness, / and to walk humbly with your God? (**Micah 6:8**)

Think about the last time you went rock climbing or hiking near a steep ledge. What were your steps like? Did you bound from point to point, giving little thought to where your feet would land? Or were you deliberate, careful, and cautious, watching nearly every step?

Walking humbly with God is rather like rock climbing, particularly like those who walk with care. *Humble* in this case means "careful" or "circumspect." In other words, if you are walking humbly with God you walk through life careful to keep God first, and your feet on the path that follows God's will.

As you leap and climb from point to point through your life's journey, be sure not to walk alone. Allow God to be your companion, and you'll always have sure feet.

Guide of my life, keep my steps sure, and walk beside me. Amen.

When the Dominoes Fall

Observe the sabbath day and keep it holy, as the LORD your God commanded you. **(Deuteronomy 5:12)**

As a kid, I loved to set up dominoes on end and topple them over. I had hundreds of them and made elaborate designs. Occasionally, though, I'd move my foot the wrong way or the cat would nudge a domino and tip one over. The dominoes would quickly fall in succession before I was ready.

In college, the youth group I led planned and held a "Domino Topple-a-Thon." We took pledges based on the number of dominoes we could set up and knock down in one chain. Essentially, we multiplied my own clumsiness by a factor of ten. Every one of the youth occasionally knocked some dominoes over.

A good domino master remembers to have breaks in the chain—places where a few dominoes are left out. Then, if one gets knocked, the entire chain isn't affected. It's easier to pick up the pieces and get going again.

Life can feel sometimes like the dominoes are falling in quick succession. One problem or action in your life leads to another, and it seems like you can't stop things from completely falling apart. That's what Sabbath is about. It's a time set aside for reflection, for putting things in perspective, for remembering who you are. Sabbath helps you deal when the dominoes in your life go down.

When my life starts to fall, God, catch me and help me stand up again. Amen.

The Happiness Pursuit

Happy are those who make / the L<small>ORD</small> their trust, / who do not turn to the proud, / to those who go astray after false gods. (Psalm 40:4)

Did you know that psychologists, economists, sociologists, and even kings study happiness? Their goal is to quantify happiness, to figure out why some people are happy and others are not.

You might have expected that those first three groups of people would study happiness, but kings? Well, at least one king, King Jigme Singye Wangchuck of Bhutan, made it his goal to have a country where happiness was experienced by everyone. And, for a while, Bhutan did rank high on happiness surveys. Then in 1998, the king made a decision: His people would be allowed to receive cable TV. Pretty quickly, the happiness index in Bhutan sank. The media frequently try to convince us that we aren't good enough as we are. Advertisers want us to feel insecure and unhappy so that we'll attempt to purchase happiness (that is, their product) at our local mall. But it's a lie to say that happiness—at least happiness that lasts—can be bought and sold.

True happiness, which is a sense of contentment, comes from living life God's way. When we follow God's desire for our life, as expressed through scripture and revealed in our prayer life, the blessing we receive is happiness. Put another way, happiness is more "gift" than "goal."

Today I put my trust in you alone, Lord.

Honor Your Parents

Honor your father and your mother, so that your days may be long in the land that the LORD your God is giving you. **(Exodus 20:12)**

This little morsel of scripture, also known as the fifth commandment, is one many people learn during their childhood. For some who learned it at that time, it may have been absorbed with a bit of extra flavor: "You'd better not disobey your parents! It says so right here in the Bible."

However, it's quite likely that it was intended for adults first and foremost. "Grown-ups, be sure to honor your own parents" is the sense in which you could hear it. But what does it mean to honor one's parents as an adult (which you, of course, are)?

There are many ways to honor your parents. You honor them by not doing certain things—getting wild at graduation or fraternity parties, wasting the money they give you for college, hanging out with friends who have little sense of right and wrong, and so on.

But you also honor them by *doing* certain things: making sure they are always cared for, living life with integrity, being respectful of their wisdom and continuing guidance in your life, making sure to stay in touch regularly (which means more than once a month!) In short, honoring your parents is a choice you make daily through your every action.

Heavenly Parent, thanks for my parents—and for those who have been like parents to me.

A Gift of Encouragement

"Therefore encourage one another and build up each other, as indeed you are doing." (1 Thessalonians 5:11)

When they look at their future, many graduates become discouraged. Some don't have a job or a clue what they'll major in. Some get concerned about being "a little fish in a big pond" (especially those who have been "the big fish in a little pond"). Some worry it will be even harder to make friends than it was before graduation. Whatever the concern, it's easy to feel as if you have little courage to face the reality set before you.

If this is true of you, I want to encourage you to seek out others who will encourage you. In 1 Thessalonians 5:11, the Greek word used for *encourage* literally means "to call alongside," a word that would have brought to mind the image of reinforcements during the heat of war. Life often feels like a battle, doesn't it? But God consistently offers us encouragement through the words of others, as well as through God's unfailing presence. If you are needing encouragement, call alongside you people who recognize your goodness, know your heart, and like you for who you are. And at the same time, be an encourager of others, like Paul and Barnabas in the New Testament. Encouragement really is a gift that keeps on giving!

Walk alongside me, Friend of the downtrodden. Amen.

Spiritual Practice: Mark Your Milestones

In ancient times, milestones literally were special carved rocks, inscribed with the image of the ruler or administrator in power at the time, that marked out distances on a road. Thus they served not only to mark distance but also to mark importance.

Today we tend to think of milestones as important moments in our lives that we have passed—like the day we lost our first tooth. But there are many others, including the days on which we were baptized, confirmed, or made significant life or faith commitments; went on a first date with someone who became a long-term boyfriend or girlfriend; lost a family member to death; and, of course, graduated. These moments should not be forgotten, because they are important points on our own life's road, and often such moments are when we can most easily see God's mark on our lives.

Try this: Get a journal with at least 365 pages. Beginning with January 1, January 2, and so forth, write the date at the top of each consecutive page, but don't indicate a particular year. (If your journal is smaller or has fewer pages, write one date at the top of the page and write the next date halfway down the page.) Use this journal to keep track of the milestones of your life by noting the year and the event, along with any other details you want to record. You might even ask a parent's or guardian's help to remember and write down the dates of significant moments from your distant past!

Get in the habit of writing in and checking your journal daily. When an anniversary of a marked milestone arrives, celebrate! Remember the importance of that moment. Give thanks to God for that milestone and for the many ways God continues to shape you as a result of it.

You Are God's Secret Ingredient

"Let me tell you why you are here. You're here to be salt-seasoning that brings out the God-flavors of this earth. If you lose your saltiness, how will people taste godliness?" (**Matthew 5:13a** *The Message*)

Quick! Name "the food senses," the kinds of tastes you have.

If you named *sweet, sour, bitter, salty,* and *umami,* you named them all. You didn't know about *umami*? Neither did I, until fairly recently.

Umami is a Japanese word that doesn't translate easily into English—thus the reason it's the odd word in the list. Roughly speaking, it means "fullness of flavor." Think of it as "abundant taste."

In Jesus' time, salt was the major preservative. In telling his hearers that they were like salt, he meant that their role was to be God's ingredient for keeping the world from getting rancid and decomposing, to help keep life from turning bad for others. That's still a powerful image! If Jesus were here today, he might call us the "*umami* of the earth," the people who experience the abundance of life with God and who want others to share that experience too. Either way, God is using you to "flavor" the world with truth and love.

Master Chef, I'm ready to spice up your world. Add me in!

Dress for Today

As God's chosen ones, holy and beloved, clothe yourselves with compassion, kindness, humility, meekness, and patience. (Colossians 3:12)

How long does it take you to pick out your clothes in the morning? A 2004 study by Sears Roebuck found the following about how long men spend on this task each day:

53 percent spend two minutes or less.
25 percent spend one minute.
12 percent spend "no time" deciding on what to wear each day.

(Sorry, women. The study didn't report on how long members of your gender devote to this daily ritual. I'll skip the easy joke that could go here.)

Paul's advice to us in Colossians is that we should all be in the "no time" category every day, but that's not because he cares one way or the other about the style and brand of clothing we grab from our closet. Instead, Paul urges us to wear the same thing: compassion, kindness, humility, gentleness, and the rest listed in the scripture above. Those are clothes that never, ever go out of fashion.

So—what are you wearing today?

May my clothing always be attractive in your eyes, God. Amen.

~~You Can't~~ You Can Go Back

Yet even now, says the LORD, / return to me with all your heart, / with fasting, with weeping, and with mourning; / rend your hearts and not your clothing. (Joel 2:12-13)

After I graduated from high school and college, I frequently wanted to go back for a visit. Occasionally, I'd do that: go to the Homecoming game, go see a former teacher, go hang out with some old friends. It was always fun, but things were never the same. Some of my old teachers had retired. I couldn't park in my "usual" space. Hardest of all for me, a close friend had died shortly after high school, and most of my other friends had moved away.

Much as we want to sometimes, we can never quite go back to the way things were. But that doesn't mean we shouldn't return sometimes to revisit our past. When we do so, we gain new perspectives, see things more clearly, understand things we couldn't have grasped in an earlier time.

A phrase found several times in the Old Testament is "Return to me." The invitation is extended to the people of Israel to follow the law again, to live in covenant with God. God's invitation to return is extended to us, too. Regardless of where we've been and what we've done, God welcomes us back with open arms. And when we return to God, we do so with a much better vision of how to live our lives anew.

I'm back, God! I'm sorry for turning from you.

Lies, Lies, and More Lies

So then, putting away falsehood, let all of us speak the truth to our neighbors, for we are members of one another. (Ephesians 4:25)

There are a lot of lies you are asked to believe, lies that are so subtle and are so much a part of our lives that we have a hard time realizing they are indeed lies. Here are three of the big ones:

1. "You can do it by yourself." God created us *in* and *for* community, not isolation. We are not self-sufficient, and we are fundamentally connected to more people on this planet than we can possibly imagine.

2. "You need to be busy." Our culture equates busy-ness with success, but they aren't the same thing. God is experienced in our stillness and in our relationships, neither of which is enhanced by busy-ness. When we seek to build community between people, we experience the fullness of life that God desires for us.

3. "You're not good enough." From beauty magazines to sports-drink ads, the message we hear again and again every day is the same: "You just don't measure up the way you are." But if you're created in the image of God, you are indeed good enough. In fact, God considers you a "very good" creation!

God, help me see through the world's lies to the truth expressed in Jesus. Amen.

Pieces of Glass

Now you are the body of Christ and individually members of it.
(1 Corinthians 12:27)

Have you ever looked closely at a stained glass window? Dozens, even hundreds of pieces are joined together by the artist in order to create an image. Viewed from a distance, one gets a sense of the whole; viewed somewhat closer, smaller details come into focus. Viewed extremely close, one sees the imperfections and color variations that give each piece richness and character. And important to appreciating the window is the one element the artist doesn't provide: light.

That's pretty much the way it is with the church, Christ's body in the world today. Viewed from a distance, one can see the many great things the community of faith does when joined together. Get a little closer, and you begin to recognize the many ways individual members pair their gifts in ministries around the community. Talk with one person, and you'll begin to hear about the stories, the tragedies, and the people who have shaped his or her life.

And through each person, God's light shines, helping everyone to be able to see the world as God does: beautiful, perfect, united.

Is your "glass" joined with others'? Are you allowing God's light to shine through you?

Light of the World, shine through all of my life so that I can brighten the dark spaces in the world. Amen.

Just Curious

For the grace of God has appeared, bringing salvation to all, training us to renounce impiety and worldly passions, and in the present age to live lives that are self-controlled, upright, and godly. (Titus 2:11-12)

Every summer, I try to learn some new, unusual skill. I've learned how to juggle, hypnotize people, read ancient Roman coins, analyze drawings people do of houses, and direct lawn-chair drill teams—just to name some of my favorites. Why? I guess I have a great curiosity about things I see others do. I want to experience a bit of what gives others joy.

During college, I noticed that a lot of students took up new behaviors. Some spent every weekend at the bars. Others went through girlfriends and boyfriends with great rapidity. Behind these actions was likely curiosity about the things others did, and the hope of finding some measure of joy in life.

Many things bring us joy, but my experience has been that what most gives people joy are not actions that are self-serving and selfish, but rather things we do for the benefit of other people: helping a friend move his stuff into a new apartment; volunteering to tutor children; treating a newcomer to dinner; sending an e-mail to a friend I haven't talked to in ages, just to say hello.

Curiosity is a gift from God, who also gave us the ability to exercise self-control when it has the potential to be harmful.

Keep me ever curious to know more about you and your world, God. Amen.

God's Communication Class

You must understand this, my beloved: let everyone be quick to listen, slow to speak ... (James 1:19)

Have you ever found yourself hopelessly lost when driving someplace that is unfamiliar to you? It happens to me quite a bit, usually because I failed to listen carefully to the directions that were given to me.

There's an old proverb that says, "God gave us two ears and one mouth, so we should listen twice as much as we speak." That's pretty good advice! In my case, I'm deaf in one ear—but that doesn't exempt me from this wise counsel.

Communication, as all students learn in any Communications 101 class, requires two parts: speaking and listening. Generally, the listening part is the most important part. Good listening is a gift we can give to others every time we are with them, because more than anything else, listening communicates to others that we value them.

Likewise, communication with God requires a lot of listening too. Our prayers should be not just filled with words, because when we forget to listen for God's voice we frequently miss out on God's direction for our lives. God already knows the desires of our hearts; what God desires is a relationship—and that requires careful listening on our part.

[Today, take a few minutes and just sit in silence, opening yourself to God.]

Spiritual Practice: Celebration

In the days and weeks surrounding your graduation, you may have gone (or you may be going) to a lot of parties, celebrating your accomplishments with friends and family. Your celebrations arise out of a sense of "goodness"—it's good to be done with classes! It's good to get a pat on the back (not to mention a twenty-dollar bill in the card!).

For Christians, celebration is a core part of our faith. The world that God created, we read in Genesis 1:31, was declared "very good" by God. Often, though, we look around at the trouble and pain in the world and doubt that's true. Lament seems more appropriate after watching the news than celebration.

But our faith is a resurrection faith. We know that the final word, the last truth, is not death, grief, and humiliation. It's joy! Our story declares that we can celebrate a joy and hope far greater than anything good or bad our world manufactures.

Celebration is not about pretending it's your birthday every day. Rather, it's about remembering that resurrection is the real heart of our faith, the perspective we choose to take when we engage all of the problems around us.

So, dance without worrying if you look foolish! Walk barefoot more often. Try strange new foods—and laugh when the make you queasy. Keep a "gladness journal" with lists of things that casue you to rejoice. Above all, "Fear not, earth! Be glad and celebrate! GOD has done great things" (Joel 2:21 *The Message*).

Genuine or Fake?

The princes of Zoan are utterly foolish; / the wise counselors of Pharaoh give stupid counsel. **(Isaiah 19:11)**

Excitedly, I ripped open my latest Internet auction-site purchase—an ancient coin of King Herod. I'd been warned by a recognized expert that the coin was probably fake, but I didn't listen, wanting to believe the seller's assurance that it was genuine and the few "experts" on a listserv who deemed it legit. Sure enough, I'd been duped. The coin was one that had been produced in large quantities twenty years ago. When I compared it later to a genuine specimen, there could be no doubt.

It's easy to be misled when we ignore wise counsel. Something sounds good to our ears, so we believe it. The source seems convincing enough, so we buy in. Counterfeit faith abounds in our world, with advice like "God will bless you with wealth if you trust him" or "It really doesn't matter what you do in life, only that you believe in Jesus." Such advice might *sound* good and true and wise, but when compared to the truth of scripture, its counterfeit nature becomes clear.

The best way to know a fake coin is to study real ones. Likewise, the best way to recognize fake faith is to get to know people with true and lasting faith that is deeply informed by scripture and a life of prayer.

Source of Truth, when I encounter counterfeit faith, help me recognize it. Amen.

Make Two Lists

Give thanks in all circumstances. **(1 Thessalonians 5:18)**

Get out a sheet of paper and pen. Really, I mean it. (I'll wait.)

OK, now make a list of the things you definitely will miss about your esteemed educational institution and your life there. Things like secret late-night conversations with a friend; shopping for new clothes for the first week of school; certain school traditions people from other schools wouldn't understand.

Give God thanks for each item on your list. It won't be hard—you might think of each of them as a blessing you have experienced. Some of these things you will experience in other ways in the future, while some other things on your list may never be a part of your life again. This is part of the way life is in God's very good world.

Now make a list of the things you won't miss a bit. Things such as cafeteria Mystery Meat; Mr. Wigitowski's economics class; losing to the school rival—four years in a row.

Look over that list, and give God thanks for each item on it. Seriously, I mean it. Everything on that list was part of your life, and these items have shaped you. Some of the things you won't miss helped develop your character or your patience in a way you can appreciate looking back on it. Other things on your list may not have been fun but you may find them to be helpful somewhere down the road. They are all a part of God's very good world.

God, may I always remember to say "Thanks!" for every part of my life.

Naturally Inclined

Now there are varieties of gifts, but the same Spirit; and there are varieties of services, but the same Lord. (1 Corinthians 12:4)

T hink back to your childhood. What did you love to do more than anything? What made your heart sing?

One woman I know spent hours as a child staring at a lake. She now works in the field of natural history. A man from my congregation would fall asleep at night clutching the vacuum cleaner at the age of two. He went on to become a mechanical engineer.

A nun in the late 1600s, Juana Inés de la Cruz, knew as a child that God had given her a talent for academic study, a pursuit that was thought of as not appropriate for women—and particularly a religious woman—of that time. Everyone discouraged her, and she even prayed that God would take her inclination away. She wrote to her bishop: "Neither the reprimands of others ... nor my own considerations ... have succeeded in making me abandon this natural impulse which God has implanted in me." (From *A Sor Juana Anthology,* trans. Alan S. Trueblood [Cambridge: Harvard University Press, 1988], as cited in the Women Speak of God curriculum from Wesley Theological Seminary)

Knowing what you've always been inclined to do is important, for often we discover that our natural impulses are gifts from God. When we do those things we are most inclined to do, our work life, our volunteer efforts, and other parts of our lives become far more rich, satisfying, and meaningful. Serving God becomes almost effortless and a complete joy. How are you using your natural inclinations for the glory of God?

Show me, God, what you have implanted in me.

Striving for Perfection

"Be perfect, therefore, as your heavenly Father is perfect."
(Matthew 5:48)

If you've ever played an instrument at a contest, performed in a play, or taken part in a speech competition, you know the pressure to be perfect. Miss a few notes or forget your lines, and a trip to the next competition might not be in your future. And worst of all, remember all the tension you felt right before you went out to face the audience or the judges?

So when people read the verse above for the first time, they may be inclined to think that being perfect is neither possible nor desirable. Who wants all that stress, right? Who can be spiritually perfect, blameless, and morally perfect?

Fortunately, this is one of those passages that don't translate perfectly into English. The Greek word for "perfect" in this case means something closer to being whole, complete, fulfilled. Its parallel in Jesus' remarks in Luke (6:36) also carries with it connotations of compassion and love. So being perfect as God is perfect means becoming wholly a person of compassion and love. Now, *that's* something worth striving for!

Perfect me, God, until I live like Jesus. Amen.

Got Patience?

The fruit of the Spirit is love, joy, peace, patience, kindness, generosity, faithfulness, gentleness, and self-control.
(Galatians 5:22-23a)

My parents lived in a "mail-in world." When they'd finish shooting a roll or cartridge of film, they'd mail it in to a company far away to be developed. In ten days or so, they'd have their pictures—usually.

I grew up in more of a "one-hour world." If I just can't wait a day or two to get my photos, I can pay a little extra and get them developed the same day. Best of all, I don't have to worry about pictures of my wife's birthday party, or some other important occasion, ending up in someone else's mailbox.

Your world is a "digital world." You can individually download your digital pictures, then instantly e-mail them to your friends (after removing all of the blemishes from your face). Isn't this a wonderful time to be alive?

There is one problem, though, with our nanosecond world: We tend to have a really hard time being patient these days. If something can't be downloaded instantly, purchased immediately, or viewed right now, we're not inclined to wait for it.

However, our faith doesn't develop instantly; our prayers are answered in God's time, and we often go through long stretches when it feels like our faith picture is out of focus. Patience is a trait we develop when we fill our life's picture with God's spirit.

God, give me patience. Amen.

A Dried-up Fortune Cookie

A cheerful heart is a good medicine, / but a downcast spirit dries up the bones. (Proverbs 17:22)

When you crack open a fortune cookie, you expect a pithy but vague message, such as "Dream your dream, and your dream will dream of you." You don't expect to see the message, "Help! I'm being held prisoner in a Chinese bakery!" Yet that humorous morsel really has been printed and put in restaurant cookies. It's great to see that the fortune-cookie company doesn't take itself too seriously.

For the life of me I don't know why, but there are a lot of dried-up Christians who have a grim image of God, a gloom-and-doom image of the future, and a glum disposition much of the time. Sometimes their words sound like an "*un*fortune cookie" message: "Don't [*fill in the blank*], or you'll be weeping and wailing in the life to come." But as you read in the Scripture from the previous devotion (Galatians 5:22-23a), one of the fruits of God's spirit is joy!

So go ahead: Laugh! Tell jokes! Watch a funny movie with friends! Blow bubbles! Let your heart be merry, for God is truly in these moments.

Giver of all that is good, thanks for ostriches and dandelions, roller coasters and cotton candy, and friends who make me smile!

Tend and Till

The LORD God took the man and put him in the garden of Eden to till it and keep it. (Genesis 2:15)

H ere's a quick trivia question for you: What's the first commandment in the Bible?

Most people are surprised that God's first instruction to anyone is to "tend and till" the garden. The instruction was given to Adam, but it was given to us too. Like Adam and Eve, you and I are set in the midst of God's beautiful creation, and we are expected to be good gardeners of it.

Now, I can't grow much of anything except dandelions in my yard, and when it comes to houseplants—well, let's just say that it once took me two months to realize that I had killed my bonsai tree! But that doesn't mean I don't take seriously my responsibility to care for God's creation.

Being a gardener, taking care of God's creation, is something you can do every day. Walk, ride your bike, or take the bus whenever possible to conserve fuel and cut down on pollution. Consider reducing your meat intake, since a diet high in fruits and vegetables requires fewer natural resources than an animal-based diet. Recycle, and don't buy stuff you don't need. You know many other ways, I'm sure. But there's one more thing you can now do as a graduate: Make sure the work you choose to do is environmentally responsible.

Creator, thanks for entrusting me with your garden! I commit to caring for your creation daily.

Spiritual Practice: Lectio Divina

No, this isn't the spiritual practice of learning foreign languages. *Lectio Divina* (pronounced lek-see-oh dee-vee-nah) is a way of slowly meditating on and opening yourself up to the riches of scripture.

As with the other spiritual practices in this book, you can (and really are encouraged to) learn much more about *Lectio Divina*, either from a book in your local library or online. There are a few ways to use this practice by yourself or with others in a group. Here's the basic process.

Step one: Choose a short passage of scripture to reflect on. If you have a daily devotional guide of some sort, you could use the daily scripture provided there.

Step two: Read the passage very slowly, savoring each word. Listen for any word or phrase that seems to stand out to you, then stay with that word or phrase. As you reflect on it, ask God to speak in the silence about its significance for your life.

Step three: Ponder the passage. Interact with God in whatever way seems right for you.

Step four: Be still and listen. Rest in God.

This process becomes especially powerful in a group, as you can have everyone share the part of the scripture that spoke to them. When you practice *Lectio Divina,* you'll be amazed at the many ways passages you have heard many times can become fresh and new.

Your First Job

From the fruit of the mouth one is filled with good things, / and manual labor has its reward. (Proverbs 12:14)

After graduating from high school, I took my first real full-time job. I was a summer maintenance worker for a Christian camp, but fixing things was rarely part of my job. Instead, I maintained the camp by cleaning showers and toilets, picking up trash, mowing, and doing many other odd jobs. It was exhausting and not particularly rewarding work; I didn't get to work with kids much, and I worked longer hours than almost everyone else on staff, but I loved the camp and I wanted other people to love it as much as I did.

Your first job after graduation may not be your ideal job either, but first jobs are important life milestones. They are places for learning how to get along with others, for developing habits such as punctuality and attention to detail, and for discovering more about what you are good at.

First jobs are also great places to practice living out your faith. You don't have to preach to your coworkers, but you do have a chance to practice being compassionate to strangers and caring with coworkers, and you have an opportunity to let the light of Christ shine through you. Doing so is a great way to thank God for the good gift of work!

So many people don't have meaningful work to do, God. I'm grateful for my job. Amen.

If Things Don't Work Out

We know that all things work together for good for those who love God, who are called according to his purpose. **(Romans 8:28)**

During my first few months as a college freshman, I worked as the computer programmer for a school bus company, creating and analyzing flowcharts and databases. The job was great, and the pay was even better.

But three months after I started, the company was sold to a much bigger company, which didn't see a need for my services and let me go. Shocked, I walked up the stairway and discovered that the business upstairs needed help. Within days, I was working as an accountant and delivery person for a florist!

The sudden job loss was just what I needed to reevaluate my major. I wasn't completely convinced computer science was where God wanted me to be, so I changed a few classes and discovered a new love: psychology.

There will be many moments when you are unsure about the decisions you've made or the direction you are taking. Possibly, the door to your future may even be slammed shut in front of you. But the good news is that these moments of doubt and frustration are times when God provides new opportunities. They also are often when we are most ready to listen for God's direction. God can turn your "flowcharts" into "flowers," too!

In the hard times of my life, Lord, help me know you're still working on me. Amen.

To the Best of Your Ability

If it is possible, so far as it depends on you, live peaceably with all.
(Romans 12:18)

Following your graduation, chances are good that in a few days, weeks, or months, your living situation is going to be very different than it is now. Maybe you'll have a roommate (or two or three), or maybe you'll be living at home but with a much different level of freedom than in the past.

Regardless of your situation, you can count on having some adjustment difficulties. Your mom might give you grief for sleeping in too late. Your roommate might spill something on your computer, then claim it was done by someone else. Others in your dorm or apartment might drive you crazy with their awful taste in music.

When your relationships get strained or tested, your true character will undoubtedly show. If you find yourself about to blow your top, stop! See the situation through the other person's eyes, and then try to treat that person as you think Jesus would. In short, choose peace.

Fill me with your peace, Gentle One, so I may be a peaceful presence for others.

Avoiding "the Freshman Fifteen"

Or do you not know that your body is a temple of the Holy Spirit within you, which you have from God, and that you are not your own? For you were bought with a price; therefore glorify God in your body.

(1 Corinthians 6:19-20)

No doubt you've heard the rumors: Many people put on an extra fifteen pounds during their first year after graduating. With all of the late-night pizzas, dozens of cafeteria options, parties, and free time for snacking, it's really no surprise.

Gaining a lot of unwanted weight is not a *fait accompli;* you *can* reverse it. But you'll need to make wise choices about your body, which is God's dwelling place. Moderation in life is the key. Decide now what you'll do to avoid the extra calories. For starters:

- Choose coffee, maybe with a little skim milk, over the extra-large caramel-mocha frappucino with whipped cream at the coffee shop.
- Let someone else have the last piece of pizza. You'll gain favor instead of weight.
- Loops-O-Fruit is not a food group. Sorry.
- Your mom was right: Veggies really are good for you!

Take care of your temple. It's yet another way to be a good steward of God's creation!

Dear God, help me to make wise choices about my body, so I can better serve you. Amen.

Add Some S P A C E

Hurry and help me; I want some wide-open space in my life! (Psalm 38:22 The Message)

IsthispagereallyhardforyoutoreadIfitsnotthenyoushouldthinkab
outgoingintothestudyofancientlanguagesAncientwritersinlangua
geslikeHebrewfrequentlydidnotusespacesintheirwritingbe
causetheparchmenttheywroteonwasveryexpensiveandwritinglike
thissavedspaceItdoesmakeunderstandingsomepassagesreallyhard
NowthinkforamomentaboutyourownlifeDoesyourlifeeverlooklik
ethisSometimeswettrytopackamillionthingsintoeverydaythinking
thatwillhelpusfeelasifwearefufilledButwhenthereisnospaceforGo
dinyourlifethingsoftengetreallyconfusingandjumbledandhardtos
ortoutWeneedpausesinourlifetomakesenseofallthatweexperience
andhearanddoNowifyouhavemadeitthisfarIhavesomegoodnewsf
oryouNotonlydoyouhavethequalityofpersistenceinyourlifebuty
oualsoknowoneofthesecretstoameaningfullife:Makespaceinyourl
ifeforGod(God always makes space for you)andyouwillfind
thatyourlifehasalotmorebreathingroom

God, I commit to putting commas, periods, and spaces in my life, so there's room for you. Amen.

A Cure for Forgetfulness

Bind them as a sign on your hand, fix them as an emblem on your forehead, and write them on the doorposts of your house and on your gates. **(Deuteronomy 6:8-9)**

If there were an award given out to the most forgetful person in the world, I'd probably receive it. Trouble is, I'd forget to go to the ceremony! I compensate for my forgetfulness by carrying an electronic organizer with me, archiving my deleted e-mails, and using a computer program that stores my notes and to-do lists.

Many people—me included—have trouble remembering to pray, study the Bible, or do other spiritual disciplines regularly. The people of ancient Israel apparently had a memory problem, too. They were constantly being reminded of their story and what God desired of them. In order to help them remember, they were instructed to basically do the equivalent of writing sticky notes— by doing things like hanging a tiny scroll at the entrance to their home (which many Jews still do today).

There are hundreds of ways you can leave yourself reminders to make your faith a more regular part of your life: bookmarks, notes in odd places, key chains, a cross in your pocket, a screensaver—all of these and more might work for you. Why not make some faith reminders for yourself today? Do it now—before you forget!

May all of life be a reminder of you, God.

Cleaning Out the Clutter

Since we have these promises, beloved, let us cleanse ourselves from every defilement of body and of spirit, making holiness perfect in the fear of God. **(2 Corinthians 7:1)**

Ever so often, it's a good idea to clean out the clutter. The junk mail piles up, clothes you haven't worn since tenth grade take up shelf space in your closet, and old candy bar wrappers get stuck under the bed. All that stuff just collects dust and makes your life more complicated. Granted, some of it might be worth something on eBay someday, but who has the space to store it until the year 2045?

It's good to clean out the clutter in our spiritual life, too. Sometimes, our heads are filled with messages about religion, faith, Christianity, or God, including things we've heard somewhere that are just plain not true and which prevent us from entering fully into the mystery that is God. Sometimes, we haven't allowed our understanding of God or Jesus to change much beyond what it was in the seventh grade. Sometimes we've developed poor Bible study habits that need to be replaced with habits more appropriate to our increased maturity. And sometimes, we just need to toss out the stuff in our lives that keeps us from a deeper relationship with God.

What's the clutter in your spiritual life? Are you ready—and do you have the courage—to toss out the trash?

Lead me, Lord—straight to the trash dump! Amen.

Spiritual Practice: Walk a Labyrinth

A labyrinth is an ancient prayer and meditation tool. It looks like a maze, but unlike a maze there is no way to get lost; there's just one path in and out. You can slowly trace the labyrinth below with a paper clip as you pray or contemplate a problem, or there are many larger examples of labyrinths and various designs available to download online. Better yet, contact churches or retreat centers in your area to see if they have a labyrinth. It's worth the hunt, because a labyrinth can help you take new steps on your spiritual journey and life path.

Everything I Need to Know About Life
I Learned at Hallmark

Each of us must please our neighbor for the good purpose of building up the neighbor. (Romans 15:2)

The title of this devotion might be overstating it a bit, but seriously ... who doesn't love getting a greeting card in the mail? You feel great knowing someone cares about you and was thinking of you, even if you're not feeling well to begin with and that's the reason you got the card.

I read a story recently about a guy who sends out thousands of birthday cards each year to friends, family, and acquaintances. People he's never even met e-mail him and ask to be added to his list, and he gladly obliges. What a great way to encourage and build up others!

Next time you browse the shelves at a greeting-card store, get an extra card or two for a friend, teacher, relative, church-staff member, or another person who wouldn't be expecting a card from you, and send it out right away with a note of your own. You'll bring joy to someone else's life, strengthen your friendship network, and feel great inside!

God, help me spread to others the joy I find in you.

Time on Your Hands

Don't waste your time on useless work, mere busywork, the barren pursuits of darkness. Expose these things for the sham they are.
(Ephesians 5:11 *The Message*)

One of the things that is hard for many graduates is time management. New college students, for example, often find they seemingly have all sorts of free time every day. Yet the number-one time students flunk out of school is during their first semester, and for a majority of them this happens because they never figure out that they need to budget their time in order to complete their homework.

New college grads sometimes struggle to figure out what to do with their evenings and weekends once they have a regular job. Suddenly, there aren't as many friends around as there were in college. Many new college graduates struggle with mild depression, loneliness, boredom, or a feeling of being lost.

In each case, it's absolutely important to remember that you don't need to make the transition alone. It's definitely OK to ask for help during times of adjustment. An older family member, a counselor, a campus minister or pastor, or a trusted professor can help you know how to be a good steward of your time. God has created us to be in relationship with one another, and those relationships become so important during times of transition.

My time is yours, and it's precious, God. Help me use it well and not waste it.

Pack a Compass

Give me your lantern and compass, give me a map, / So I can find my way to the sacred mountain, to the place of your presence.

(Psalm 43:3 *The Message*)

If you are on your way to college, be sure to pack a small compass. At many large campuses, it can be really tough to find your way around. So find the tallest landmark on campus, then find another common building on a north-south axis with your selected landmark. Then, you'll always have an easy way to get oriented anywhere on campus!

But there's another reason to carry a compass, even if you are one of those lucky people who have a better sense of direction due to a greater concentration of iron in their nose. A compass serves as a great reminder to be guided by "true north" as you make your way through life. Most people choose other things to guide their life, like the clock or their Palm Pilot or their wallet. But being guided by True North, the core truths you have learned from Jesus, will always ensure that you know the directions you should take when you feel lost.

I'm pointing myself in your direction, Jesus. Fill me with your presence. Amen.

How Many Bars Do You Have?

He gives power to the faint, / and strengthens the powerless.
(Isaiah 40:29)

Have you ever stopped to think about how many gadgets now have "bars" to measure their remaining power or signal strength? iPods, laptops, PDAs, and cell phones are among the common items many graduates carry with them on a daily basis. Woe to the person who forgets to check the bar on her laptop before class or an important meeting!

I sometimes wish I were equipped with a bar. If I had an energy bar, I would be more likely to recharge before I'm completely exhausted. If I had a signal bar, I'd probably be more attuned to the places in my life where I have wandered away from God. But of course I have no such visible guides to the state of my physical or spiritual power, so I have to do something else: I have to know myself.

That sounds simple enough, but a lot of individuals have a good deal of trouble really knowing who they are. It starts with knowing and really understanding that you are a beloved child of God. This one basic yet profound fact needs to be remembered every day, for it's the fountain from which a healthy spirituality and great power flows.

Fill me with your Holy Spirit, God, so I will have power to spare. Amen.

Thanks a Lot!

I do not cease to give thanks for you as I remember you in my prayers.
(Ephesians 1:16)

If this book was a gift, I hope you've already said thanks to the person who gave it to you. Presumably, you have finished writing thank-you notes to everyone who gave you a graduation gift. (If not, it's definitely not too late to get started.)

Gratitude for all you have and all you are is key to a life of joy. What's more, expressing your gratitude sincerely is a great way to give joy to others.

Why not spend the next several days writing thank-you notes (yes, actual handwritten notes) to the people who have been so important the past few years? Tell your parents or guardians how much you appreciate their many sacrifices on your behalf; tell your grandparents how thankful you are for being great parents to your parents.

Tell your favorite teachers how much you learned from them that you couldn't fit on the evaluation form; tell a Sunday school teacher how he or she changed your life by sharing his or her faith with you; tell a boss what you learned about work from your experience on the job; tell a friend what you'll remember most about the time you spent together.

As you write each note, offer a prayer of thanks to God for these great people in your life!

Thank you, God, for _____ and for all this person has done for me. Amen.

Bitter or Better?

Bear with one another and, if anyone has a complaint against another, forgive each other; just as the Lord has forgiven you, so you also must forgive. (Colossians 3:13)

It just wouldn't go away. I'd taken my work boot off twice searching for a rock inside, but I just didn't find one that would have caused the twinge of pain I kept feeling. Finally, on the third try—a few hours after I first felt the pain—I discovered the source.

A nail was embedded in my shoe. It was just a short little tack, so short that it poked through the insole only when I stepped on it just right. But it was there, and I was slowly getting agitated as a result.

This is not unlike what happens to us when someone hurts us. In my case, it was a new girlfriend whom I'd always wanted to date but never had the guts to ask out. We finally started dating shortly after graduation, and things were going well, but just three days later, without any explanation, she started going out with another guy. Ouch! That "little nail" still stings a bit, even years later.

I've learned through the years that we always have two choices in life: to grow bitter or to grow better. Harboring a grudge is a good way to grow bitter. Pulling the nail out—forgiving those persons who hurt us—is the way to grow better.

Forgive my sins, Lord, just as I forgive others. Amen.

The Big Question

Beloved, let us love one another, because love is from God; everyone who loves is born of God and knows God. (1 John 4:7)

At the end of every day, there may be no better question to ask of ourselves than, "Did I grow in love today?" For love is the nature of God, and our love is the best response to being loved.

Love isn't just something restricted to your most intimate relationships—or even to a good cup of java. Rather, love is something you can express in numerous ways in all of your encounters. Celebrating life is a form of love that comes from gratitude to God for the gift of life. "Carefrontation" (confrontation with care) can show someone that you love them but do not approve of some harmful action. Reverence and awe, forgiveness, humor, compassion, helpfulness, attentive listening, creativity, and loyalty are all other possible expressions of love.

You are loved by God. Believe it, for it's true. God's love has the power to change your life—and others' lives through you.

God, fill me with your love, and show me how to serve my neighbors. Amen.

Spiritual Practice: Doubt

A lot of Christians grow up believing that the opposite of *faith* is *doubt*. It's as if there are spiritual equations that must be accepted as being just as true as the Pythagorean theorem: faith = good; doubt = bad. Possibly this idea springs from Jesus' words to Thomas after the Resurrection: "Put your finger here and see my hands. Reach out your hand and put it in my side. Do not doubt but believe" (John 20:27), as well as the fact that too often faith is simplistically defined as "believing something for which there is no direct proof."

Doubt, however, is not a barrier to faith, but the threshold to it. When we ponder, reflect, and ask serious questions about our doubts, we move deeper into the mystery of God. We are forced to search for new meanings, new answers that make sense, and new hope for living. In our doubts, we discover the ways God is transforming and changing our hearts. We discover that the opposite of faith is actually *fear,* which causes us to stop doing God's work in the world, and to lose our faith in one another and in ourselves. We discover that faith has more to do with fidelity and trust than it does with right belief.

So go ahead—have doubts! Have lots of them, even! But then, be willing to pursue them with diligence and effort and an honest search for something deeper.

In the Painful Moments

But I am lowly and in pain; / let your salvation, O God, protect me.
(Psalm 69:29)

Grief. Loss. Pain. Homesickness. Disappointment. Sadness. Not all emotions following graduation are happy ones. Some days—maybe now, maybe a few weeks from now—you'll feel some variation on emotions like these ...

... when you realize all your friends are gone and you're still in the same place

... at the moment you wonder if "long-distance relationship" really means "long-shot relationship"

... the first time you get sick and Mom or Dad isn't there to check in on you

... when a family birthday or special event comes around, but you can't be there to join in the fun.

It's important to let yourself feel deeply at moments like these, and not to pretend that nothing is wrong. Life is lonely and even painful at times, and our emotions in those moments are necessary and normal. At these times, faith won't make things instantly better; I'm sorry to be the bearer of that bad news. But faith will help you to know that you'll make it through the rough times. God is always present, comforting and sustaining us, and reminding us that hope is possible.

Dear Comforting One, when I am suffering and in pain, rescue me by your saving power. Amen.

Take the Shot

No matter how many times you trip them up, God-loyal people don't stay down long; / Soon they're up on their feet, while the wicked end up flat on their faces. **(Proverbs 24:16 *The Message*)**

Basketball legend Michael Jordan once said, "I've missed more than 9,000 shots in my career. I've lost almost 300 games. Twenty-six times, I've been trusted to take the game-winning shot and missed. I've failed over and over and over again in my life. And that is why I succeed."

Watching Michael Jordan play basketball was truly amazing. It always seemed like every shot went in with a swoosh, like every graceful move was perfection on earth. But Jordan was much more realistic about his abilities. He acknowledged his failures, yet he also knew that his failures were not what defined him.

If you've been (un)lucky enough to make it to today without significant failures, you're definitely overdue. Odds are good that you're going to make many mistakes from here on out. That's true of every area in our life, including our spiritual life. We frequently fall short of where God calls us to be.

But our failures are not what define us in God's eyes. God loves us and forgives us, so we don't need to be ruled by our own "missed shots." You don't need to be perfect to get through life successfully, and you don't need a perfect faith to make game-winning shots for God.

Coach of my life, fill me with the courage to take the shots available today. Amen.

Fiery Words, Friendly Words

And the tongue is a fire. The tongue is placed among our members as a world of iniquity; it stains the whole body, sets on fire the cycle of nature, and is itself set on fire by hell. (James 3:6)

When I eat fire (yes, I really can), I always end a show with my favorite trick. I take two torches—one lit, one unlit—and transfer the fire from one to the other by lighting my tongue on fire momentarily. It looks pretty cool, and if I do it correctly I don't get burned in the process. (However, as they say, don't try this at home.)

For me, this trick is a visual representation of the message in James 3:6. Our tongues can be filled with fire. When we yell at or speak sharp words to someone, our words can quickly ignite a fire within that person as well. The result: two flaming torches instead of one, both in danger of burning others.

Of course, our words can also be used to calm, soothe, heal, comfort, encourage, build up, and warm the hearts of others. Words that do this also spread from person to person, for they help contribute to a person's growth.

Throughout the day, stop and ask yourself if you're a fire-starter intent on burning others or one who plants the seeds of restoration. Your words could be the best gift others receive all day.

God, may the words of my mouth and the meditations of my heart be acceptable in your sight.

Wise as Andy

"See, I am sending you out like sheep into the midst of wolves; so be wise as serpents and innocent as doves." **(Matthew 10:16)**

In college, a guy on my floor named Andy was exceptionally clever. Once, when a philosophy professor gave the class the assignment of writing a persuasive essay, Andy signed his name to a piece of paper that read, "I deserve an F on this paper." When Andy got his paper back and F was indeed the grade marked in red, he argued that the professor had indeed been persuaded, and thus he deserved a better grade. The professor changed Andy's grade to an A! (Here again, you probably shouldn't try this at home.)

We usually don't think of Jesus as being cunning, but biblical scholars are increasingly sure this was one of his qualities. In a world where the Romans were in charge, Jesus encouraged his followers to act in wise and clever ways. That's good advice for us today, too. Our world isn't always supportive of the kind of life Jesus calls us to live. Justice and compassion are not the typical highest values of government or the business world. To be faithful all of the time frequently takes the wisdom to know the ways the world works, and to use them with the kind of cleverness my philosophical friend did.

Grant me cleverness and wisdom, Holy Spirit, so I can follow Jesus when it seems impossible. Amen.

Be a Windchanger

We must no longer be children, tossed to and fro and blown about by every wind of doctrine. **(Ephesians 4:14a)**

Have you ever been around someone who lived their life by wetting their finger and holding it up to see which way the wind was blowing? Some people seem to be unable to make a decision for themselves and instead just follow the hottest trend. Others aren't good at sticking to their principles and values, instead choosing to take part in whatever their friends do.

Rather than being blown about by the winds of popularity, Christians are called to be "windchangers," people who move others. Your actions, your letters to Congress, your whole life can be the wind that changes the world for good and for God. Fill yourself with God's spirit, then breathe into the world the breath of fresh air we all need.

Breathe on me, breath of God, until I am wholly yours. Amen.

Stupid Fears

I spent my whole life until college in Wisconsin, but I went to college in Illinois. You'd think that would be an easy thing to keep separate, right? Yet the very first time I opened my mouth to talk on the air as a DJ for my college radio station, I found myself saying, "This is WONC, Naperville, Wisconsin."

My "babysitter," the older student assigned to teach me how to "run the board," literally fell off his chair with laughter. I'm sure my face was more cardinal-red than the school mascot, but what was worse was I had a new fear that every time I'd open my mouth, I'd say something stupid.

Just about everyone has a "stupid" fear, something like, *I'll look stupid if I don't know where my classes are. I'll look stupid if I wear the wrong thing to work. I'll sound stupid if I don't know how to answer her questions. If I don't know what I want to do with my life, everyone will think I'm stupid.* When our fear takes over, then sploosh! Like Peter, who could walk on the water until he became afraid, into the water we go (Matthew 14:27-31).

Jesus' message to us is "Fear not, for I am with you." Will we make mistakes? Of course. Will we make fewer of them over time? Of course. Are we capable of walking on water? Absolutely!

Calm my fears, Jesus, calm my fears.

Pitch Any Tents?

Then Peter said to Jesus, "Rabbi, it is good for us to be here; let us make three dwellings, one for you, one for Moses, and one for Elijah." (Mark 9:5)

You know those times when you just don't want a moment to end? Whether it's the perfect date, an incredible trip, or a laughter-filled party with friends, our tendency is to want to remain there. We wish we could just "pitch a tent" and camp out at that moment in time, like Peter at Jesus' transfiguration.

We feel that way because deep down we know things won't be the same again. When we go home after a long time away, our friends, parents, and towns will have changed. We like the comfort and security of the mountaintop experience, but we can't stay there.

In what areas of your life is your tendency to pitch a tent rather than setting out on faith?

Liberating God, help me let go of those things I need to but can't. Amen.

Spiritual Practice: Give

Most people are surprised when they learn that money is the most frequent human topic in the Bible. Somehow, money doesn't seem like a spiritual issue; it's just part of our daily existence, something we all need in order to survive, right?

Yet we know money causes us stress, disrupts our relationships, consumes our thoughts, and sometimes causes us to act in violent ways. Far too many people—over a billion—live on less than a dollar a day. A few hundred millionaires own the same wealth as the world's poorest 2.5 billion people combined. Clearly, our world has a spiritual crisis when it comes to money. And that was true in Jesus' day, when he said, "No one can serve two masters; for a slave will either hate the one and love the other, or be devoted to the one and despise the other. You cannot serve God and wealth" (Matthew 6:24).

The giving of our money sometimes seems like an impossibility when we have so many bills and so little money. And sometimes in our lives, it probably is. But often—and perhaps even *usually*—we do have some disposable income. For example, we are able to choose not to spend two dollars on a vending-machine soda when other options are available.

Start practicing a life of giving to charity and to God. Start small, even if it's just a few cents each week. Gradually, give more. As you do so, you'll discover that the generous life is a joyous, meaningful, and God-filled life.

The Patience of a Cocklebur

So let us not grow weary in doing what is right, for we will reap at harvest-time, if we do not give up. **(Galatians 6:9)**

Wanna know a secret? You're going to have times in your life when your faith seems weak, when your doubts are greater than your beliefs, when your service doesn't seem to matter, and when you have more questions than answers.

Maybe that's not such a secret, but it is a truth that doesn't get talked about much in a lot of churches or by a lot of Christians. When you don't "feel" like you are connected to God, what should you do?

The best thing to do is to keep practicing your faith until the feelings and the certainty return. In all relationships—with people and with God—we have times when we don't feel very connected, but that doesn't mean we should quit the relationship.

Sometimes it can take a while. We can learn much about patience from nature. The sticky seedpod of the cocklebur contains two seeds, which germinate in different years. One germinates during the first spring or summer, and although the second generally germinates in the second or third year, it can remain viable for eight years! Because persistence is built into the plant, when the conditions are right, the seeds will germinate.

When I want to give up on you, God, speak to me words of patience. Amen.

Our True Nature

Now you are the body of Christ and individually members of it.
(1 Corinthians 12:27)

A recent high-school graduate, when asked what she had learned in the year since graduation, shared with me two things. First, "Don't rely on anyone, because if you want something done you have to do it yourself," and second, "Get to know as many people as possible, for you never know what you might learn from them." These are good pieces of advice. We want to be independent, and we often do need to take responsibility for our own lives. And of course it's good to learn from others.

Yet on a deeper level, both of these comments underscore a self-centeredness that is not in keeping with the Christian understanding of the body of Christ. Our tradition emphasizes that we are interdependent people who truly do need each other. What we learn from others is important not because it benefits us but because it helps us to better help one another. Our true nature in Christ is one of interconnectedness, not separateness or independence.

Reread all of 1 Corinthians 12, and ask yourself, "In what ways have I been thinking or acting as if I'm disconnected from the whole body?"

Keep me connected to other Christians, O God of all earth's people. Amen.

Put Worry to Rest

"And can any of you by worrying add a single hour to your span of life?" (Luke 12:25)

An old farmer's aphorism suggests a way of life for all of us: *Live simply. Love generously. Care deeply. Speak kindly. Leave the rest to God.*

That last part is for many people the tough one. Some think that means they can shirk their responsibility for everything from studying for a test ("Dear Lord, please help me get an A on this test that I forgot about...") to caring for those who are poor ("The worse things get, the sooner Jesus will return!"). Others worry about many things that are out of their control, in the past, or simply facts of life. It's hard to "let go and let God" if you're filled with worry.

"Leaving the rest to God" means neither of these things. Instead, it means living in a relationship of trust. God trusts you'll do what you can. Trust God with the rest.

Loving God, I trust you. Amen.

Choose a Church Family

Let us not give up meeting together, as some are in the habit of doing, but let us encourage one another—and all the more as you see the Day approaching. (Hebrews 10:25 NIV)

Few things can help you in your post-graduation transition like finding a good church or campus ministry to join. There you'll find a community of people like you who have similar struggles and seek fun, friendship, and faith. But with so many churches and faith-based groups around, how does one choose?

Start with those that are closest to the tradition you grew up in, so you'll initially feel more rooted and connected with your friends and family back home. Then, listen carefully to everything you hear. Is the primary message one of fear or hope, sin or forgiveness, guilt or grace and love? Do you feel pressured to become just like the people in the group, or do you feel set free to love, worship, and serve God in a way that is uniquely you? Are you being asked to check your brain at the door, or are you encouraged to pursue difficult questions and ideas?

You may be tempted to just go where your friends go, and that's OK. But why not encourage your circle of friends to explore the various options with you? Somewhere, there's a "festival of friends" just waiting to welcome you with open arms and open hearts!

I need a community in which to grow spiritually, God. Help me discern where I can find a congregation or group with healthy, grace-filled faith.

Concrete or Clay?

Don't be selfish; don't live to make a good impression on others. Be humble, thinking of others as better than yourself. **(Philippians 2:3 NLT)**

W hen I was young, I always wanted to press my hands on or write my name in a fresh slab of poured concrete. At the time, it seemed like something I could do to make a permanent mark on the world. Now, though, I prefer making impressions in clay. It's fun to shape and carve the clay into one thing, then squish it and start over. If I don't like an impression I've made, I can always begin anew.

Likewise, when you go out into the world to pursue work or your higher education, you'll have plenty of opportunities to make impressions on others. Others will also constantly be making impressions on you. Seek to be like clay, not concrete. Remember that if you somehow make a bad first impression with someone, it's possible—with some work, of course—to make a new impression. At the same time, question your first impressions of others. Everyone is displaced when they leave home for the first time, and that can cause anyone to act in strange ways.

Above all, strive to make—as well as carry in your heart— only impressions that are based on love. It's exactly that kind of impression that God has made in us!

Holy Potter, mold and shape me. Amen.

Experiencing Information Overload?

When you pass through the waters, I will be with you; / and through the rivers, they shall not overwhelm you. (Isaiah 43:2)

One of the greatest challenges you will face in life is information overload. It's the anxiety-filled feeling when everything from the number of blue-jean choices to the varieties of music on iTunes gets to be too overwhelming. Who can keep up when, experts estimate, the information "river" doubles every two years or less?

The key to survival, psychologists suggest, is to simplify and focus your life. For example, become an expert at just one search engine. Have "data fast days" when you avoid all electronic media. Concerned about all the problems in the world? Pick one to focus on, then put your energy into learning about it and applying your unique gifts toward positive solutions.

So that I don't add to your information overload now, I'll encourage you to research the topic more on your own. Above all, keep your relationship with Jesus the central focus of your life.

Source of Peace, when things get overwhelming, protect me and keep me from going under.

Is Jesus Nuts? He's Driving Me Crazy!

When many of his disciples heard it, they said, "This teaching is difficult; who can accept it?" (John 6:60)

I'll be honest: There are days I wake up and think Jesus is nuts. His teachings seem impossible to live out in my day sometimes—actually, many times. He wasn't exactly known for hanging out with reputable people. His actions seem rather outrageous, and they did get him killed at about age thirty-three, after all. The disciples, those who knew him best, are portrayed as frequently clueless or confused. If they couldn't understand him, what chance do I have?

Yet Jesus offers this promise to his disciples when he notices they think he's crazy: "It is the spirit that gives life; the flesh is useless. The words that I have spoken to you are spirit and life" (John 6:63).

It's that "spirit and life" thing that keeps me trying to follow Jesus. Call me nuts, but I'm sticking with Jesus, and I encourage you to do the same. It's the only promise I know of that's still true after two thousand years.

Jesus, fill me with your abundant life.